Original title:
The Innovation Instinct

Editor: Jessica Elisabeth Luik
Author: Lan Donne
ISBN HARDBACK: 978-9916-86-270-4
ISBN PAPERBACK: 978-9916-86-271-1

Scripts of Tomorrow

In the quiet dawn of dreams
The ink begins to flow
Scripts of tomorrow gleam
Their secrets we'll soon know.

Between the stars and sand
Stories yet to write
In our grasp, they stand
Futures bold and bright.

Whispers from the past
Speak of what's to come
Shadows that we cast
Leave echoes where we're from.

With courage, we will face
The unknown paths ahead
In every hopeful trace
Our spirits will be led.

Lines of fate entwine
In tales of joy and sorrow
Yesterday and now combine
In scripts we shape tomorrow.

Eureka's Embrace

In silence, dreams ignite the night,
A whisper calls the stars to light.
Mysteries weave through skies afar,
Guiding minds to where you are.

From shadows rise the sparks of thought,
Invention birthed from what is sought.
As dawn unfolds its golden lace,
We find ourselves in Eureka's Embrace.

Pioneering Hearts

Led by love and courage strong,
We journey paths where dreams belong.
With every step, the future starts,
In the rhythm of pioneering hearts.

Through trails unknown, we bravely tread,
By hopes and visions, we are led.
United by an ardent fire,
We weave a world of high aspire.

Quantum of Change

Particles in dance unseen,
Merge and part in realms serene.
In the chaos, patterns grow,
Quantum whispers softly flow.

Threads of fate in light's embrace,
Form the tapestry of space.
Change the constant, never still,
Time moves forward by sheer will.

Revolution's Rhythm

Drums of change beat loud and clear,
A call to action, voices near.
Echoing through silent halls,
Revolution's rhythm calls.

Steps in unison, hearts aligned,
A future brightened, undefined.
Together, we shall rise and climb,
To the cadence of our time.

Mind's Evolution

From sparks of thought, new worlds begin,
In shadows deep, in sunlight's grin.
Ideas sprout where doubts had lain,
In endless streams, through joy and pain.

Each question asked, each answer sowed,
In fertile minds, the future's code.
Through time's embrace, we weave our lore,
As wisdom grows, forevermore.

Blueprints of Change

On parchment frail, new dreams are drawn,
Through night's embrace, and breaking dawn.
Each line a hope, each curve a plea,
For what could come, for what might be.

Foundations laid with care and might,
Constructing futures, clean and bright.
In every pulse, in every stride,
The march of change, our constant guide.

Whispers of Progress

In silent winds, the future speaks,
In hopeful tones, through valleys, peaks.
A murmured hope, a fervent prayer,
For steps untried, for challenges rare.

Through ancient halls, through modern streets,
Progress whispers, never retreats.
In every breath, a promise made,
Together strong, through light and shade.

Wings of Invention

Beneath the sky, where dreams take flight,
Innovators chase the night.
With every leap, with every bound,
New wonders rise, new thoughts unbound.

In hands that mold and minds that dream,
The future flows, a constant stream.
With wings of thought, beyond the norm,
We rise anew, in endless form.

Technological Symphony

Humming wires and circuits glow,
Silicon dreams in vibrant flow.
Digital worlds we build and mend,
On binary paths, our visions extend.

The code, a song both soft and grand,
Echoes through a shimmering land.
Machines and minds, a fusion rare,
Crafting tomorrows, crystal and fair.

Keys and screens in rhythmic tread,
Compose the future on which we tread.
An orchestra of bits and bytes,
Radiant dawn through endless nights.

Seeds of Advancement

In the soil of thought we plant,
Seeds of vision, dreams we chant.
Each idea a sprouting tree,
Branching towards what we can be.

Nurtured by the light of quest,
Watered by our hope and zest.
New horizons come to view,
From each sapling that we grew.

In the garden of the wise,
Innovation never dies.
Seeds of progress, firm and bright,
Flourish in collective light.

Spark of Future

A spark ignites in curious minds,
Lighting paths the present blinds.
In the forge of dreams and thought,
Future's shape and form are wrought.

With each flicker, shadows flee,
Revealing what is yet to be.
Hope and wisdom intertwine,
Guiding stars in cosmic line.

Boundaries fade, a distant mist,
Innovations coexist.
In the spark, our fate is spun,
A journey rich has just begun.

Echoes of Tomorrow

Whispers of what is yet to come,
Linger softly, one by one.
Echoes of a future day,
Float on breezes, light and gay.

Every sound a hint and clue,
Of a world grand and new.
In the distance, undefined,
Tomorrow's call, gentle, kind.

Resonances of dreams unborn,
Through the veil of twilight, torn.
From today's silence bright and stern,
Echoes guide us as we learn.

Boundless Potential

In seeds of thought, our futures lay,
Rich soils of hope, we find our way;
With every dawn, horizons new,
Boundless potential, dreams ensue.

Strength unseen fuels every stride,
Within our hearts, ambitions bide;
In moments still, the fire burns,
To skies unknown, our spirits yearn.

Through trials faced and mountains high,
We lift our gaze, embrace the sky;
Each challenge met, our spirits soar,
Unleashing worth, forevermore.

Pulse of Creation

In the heart of silence, whispers birth,
Songs of stars, the pulse of earth;
Nature’s brush, with vibrant hue,
Paints the dawn, in morning dew.

Rivers dance in ceaseless flow,
Mountains rise with ancient glow;
In fields of green, the earth renews,
Life's endless dance, a cosmic muse.

From seeds to trees, in cycles spun,
Every end a new begun;
In every leaf, creation's breath,
Life's gentle pulse defying death.

Dreams Transformed

In silent nights, where whispers dream,
Visions cast on moonlight's beam;
The seeds of hope in darkness sown,
Transforms to life, a world unknown.

With every star, a wish is made,
In heart's deep well, these dreams cascade;
The dawn arrives, with colors bright,
Awakens realms in morning light.

Through shadows deep and trials vast,
Dreams are forged, they hold steadfast;
In each heartbeat, a promise rings,
Dreams transformed, take flight on wings.

Horizons Reimagined

Beneath the skies, where dreams take flight,
New horizons rise in twilight;
Imagination takes the helm,
Guiding souls through mystic realm.

With strokes of light and shades of gray,
We reimagine paths each day;
In every glance, potential seeps,
With every step, a vision leaps.

Through clouds that part in morning’s grace,
We find anew our destined place;
Horizons vast, in mind's embrace,
Create anew the world's face.

Dawn of Discoveries

With the morning's first blush we stride anew,
Paths uncharted, skies of endless blue.
Whispers of wonders, just out of sight,
Brave hearts venture into the light.

Echoes of ages guide our quest,
In nature's secrets, we find our best.
Every dawn a promise, each step a find,
In the dawn of discoveries, truth we bind.

Margins of maps where dragons lay,
Unveil horizons that beckon the day.
Courageous spirits break the mold,
In new dawns, legends unfold.

Artists of Aspiration

In every stroke, a dream unfurls,
Colors dance and passions swirl.
Canvas captures heart's pure flight,
Artists' hands bring dark to light.

Brushes wielded with a grace,
Imagination finds its place.
Each creation sparks a flame,
Art and soul are one, not tame.

Visions born in whispered hues,
Ambitions sketched in varied views.
Painters, poets, sculptors bold,
Artists of aspiration, stories told.

Echoes in Silicon

Amidst the hum of circuits bright,
Voices whisper through the night.
Binary beats, a rhythmic tide,
In silicon's heart, dreams reside.

Data dances in patterns clear,
Chasing shadows, casting fear.
Lines of code in perfect flow,
Crafting futures we barely know.

Machines that think, that feel, that learn,
In silicon's embrace, they turn.
Echoes eternal, progress rings,
In this symphony, innovation sings.

Future's Forge

From molten ideas, futures are cast,
In the forge where ambitions last.
Fire of vision, tempered mind,
In the smithy of time, fate's designs.

Dreams are alloyed in hardened steel,
With every strike, a new reveal.
Plans and hopes, timeless shards,
Crafted here in destiny's yards.

Brotherhood of builders strong,
Hymns of progress, age-long song.
In this crucible, bright and bold,
Future's forge, our tales unfold.

Quantum Leaps

Particles dance in a cosmic ballet,
Invisible threads weave night into day.
Reality whispers, secrets unseen,
In realms of the tiniest, who reign supreme.

Energy quivers in a boundless sea,
Possibilities reign, wild and free.
Time bends like willow in quantum fields,
Nature reveals what future conceals.

Imagination's Forge

Spark of thought in the blankest of nights,
Forging dreams from ethereal lights.
Minds as anvil, hearts as fire,
Creating worlds, climbing higher.

Ideas spark in a passionate storm,
From chaos, visions start to form.
Unseen hammers shape the unseen,
Crafting realms in dark and between.

Chains of Revolution

Hearts beat hard in the throes of change,
Bound by dreams of a world rearranged.
Voices rise, a chorus loud,
Breaking free from the darkest cloud.

Chains of old, rusted and weak,
Crushed by those who freedom seek.
Revolution rides on wings of steel,
A future bright, a fate to seal.

Whirlwind of Ideas

In the storm of thought, chaos reigns,
Conceptual tides, breaking chains.
Mind's tempest, forever turning,
Burning bright, ceaselessly yearning.

Whirlwind gathers fragments of light,
Forming patterns in darkest night.
Ideas alight as stars above,
Guiding paths, stories of love.

Illuminated Paths

In shadows deep where fears reside,
A glimmer sparks, a light inside.
Each step we take, a mystery,
Unveiling paths of destiny.

Through winding roads and forests wild,
Guided by the heart's own child.
Courage born from whispered dreams,
A soul's adventure, endless themes.

Stars above and earth below,
In twilight's kiss, direction flows.
Trust the night and greet the morn,
With every dawn, new hope is born.

Machinations of Growth

Beneath the soil, within the seed,
Lies potential, faith, and creed.
From darkened depths to skyward flight,
Life emerges, seeking light.

Seasons turn and rivers wind,
Time's embrace, so gentle, kind.
Lessons learned in sun and rain,
Strength in patience, growth in gain.

Whispered winds on leaves bestow,
Silent tales of how we grow.
Roots entwine in earth's embrace,
Witnesses to nature's grace.

Mind Over Matter

When doubt and fear cloud judgment's eye,
Inner strength propels us high.
Beyond the limits they have set,
Boundless realms of mind are met.

Resilience in the face of strife,
Shapes the fabric of our life.
Thoughts and will align in fire,
Manifest our heart's desire.

In the quiet, wisdom's found,
Breaking free from tethered ground.
Mind can soar, unchained, anew,
Dreams transform to paths in view.

Uncharted Concepts

In realms where thought and wonder blend,
New ideas begin, ascend.
Uncharted concepts built in mind,
We explore, and truth we find.

Through the labyrinths of the brain,
Innovation, unconstrained.
Boundaries pushed, horizons wide,
In each notion, worlds collide.

Brush the edges of the known,
Craft the future, seeds are sown.
Creation birthed in abstract form,
Rides the crest of concept's storm.

Alchemy of Ideas

In caverns deep where thoughts reside,
Dreams and fears forever bide,
Whispers turn like leaves in fall,
Echoes dance from wall to wall.

Minds converge like rivers' flow,
Lighting paths where shadows grow,
Secrets speak in silent rhyme,
Crafting tales that span through time.

Wisps of wisdom, flickers bright,
Guide us through the endless night,
Mapping realms unseen, unknown,
Where seeds of genius are sown.

Surge of the Novel

Pages turned by eager hands,
Legends born in distant lands,
Words ignite a boundless sea,
Of worlds unknown to you and me.

Inky black, the printed trail,
Heroes rise and villains fail,
Each new chapter, heartbeats race,
In written thoughts, we find our place.

Journeys carved in paper's breath,
Life beyond both life and death,
Endless tales for minds to breed,
Endless thirst for more to read.

Infinite Trails

Wandering paths that never end,
Twists and turns around each bend,
Footprints left yet never seen,
In forests deep and valleys green.

Sunlight filters through the mist,
Guiding those who choose to list,
To trails crossed by old and new,
Bound by fate, though followed few.

Songs of winds and whispers pure,
Echoes of what we endure,
In this journey, hearts set sail,
Upon these infinite trails.

Inventor's Call

Gears and cogs of dreams unspun,
Echoes of a tale begun,
Sparks igniting in the night,
Chasing dawn with newfound light.

Blueprints etched in vision clear,
Crafted by a mind sincere,
Born from thoughts that twist and turn,
Fires of creation burn.

Voices whisper, shadows fall,
Answering the inventor’s call,
Paths unknown, yet hearts aligned,
Future's promise intertwined.

Future in Hand

In the twilight of dreams we stand,
Paths of hope through time unplanned.
A tapestry of stars to weave,
Infinite potential we conceive.

With courage as our guiding thread,
Through shadows dark, a light is spread.
Innovate, create, and strive,
The pulse of progress kept alive.

Wisdom anchors, vision soars,
Beyond horizon, endless doors.
Chart the course with steady grace,
In unity, our futures trace.

Mindscapes Unfurled

Voyages through the realms of thought,
Where dreams and wonder can be sought.
Landscapes painted with the mind,
Mysteries in truth confined.

In fields of ideation's bloom,
Imagination finds its room.
Beyond the tangible and known,
In mindscapes wild, our souls are flown.

Ideas whisper, thunder loud,
Breaking through the common shroud.
A symphony of unseen sights,
Illumination in the night.

Revolution Hearts

In every beat a fire’s start,
A revolution born of heart.
Voices rise and chains will rend,
A cry for justice, worlds to mend.

The power of the people's fire,
A force of change that won't retire.
From ashes, new beginnings rise,
Empowerment in unity's prize.

Through struggle, strength and will combined,
Echoes of freedom sharply defined.
A future carved by hands of many,
In revolution hearts find plenty.

Genesis of Thought

From silence springs the spark's conceive,
The genesis of thoughts we weave.
Cradled in the mind's embrace,
Ideas are born, begin their race.

A whisper in the calmest air,
In every question answers dare.
Possibilities unfold,
In knowledge, wisdom has its hold.

Seed of insight, vast and deep,
In fertile minds, they grow and leap.
Through seeking hearts and searching eyes,
The genesis of thought withstands all skies.

Wonders Unfurled

The morning sun begins to rise,
A glowing orb in lavender skies,
Birds sing songs in joyous reprise,
Nature’s beauty, a cherished prize.

Mountains wrapped in misty swirls,
Rivers flow in graceful twirls,
Leaves dance with the breeze’s swirls,
In the heart, wonders unfurled.

Cascading falls and emerald wood,
Seas of flowers understood,
In this tranquil, sacred mood,
Time stands still, as if it should.

Each dawn brings a canvas new,
With colors bright and pure, true,
Exploring all in varied hue,
Life’s endless wonders to pursue.

In moments quiet, senses find,
The boundless magic of the mind,
Unseen bonds that freely bind,
Wonders unfurled, in us defined.

Vanguard Visions

A spark ignites the dreams in flight,
Ideas born in quiet night,
Eyes that pierce through shade and light,
They guide us with their vanguard might.

Through realms of thought, they chase the stars,
Breaking chains and bending bars,
Charting courses near and far,
Vanguard visions where they are.

Innovations bright as dawn,
From minds that dare to ponder on,
They lead where inspiration's drawn,
A path towards horizons gone.

With courage wrapped in wisdom old,
They shape the future, bright and bold,
Stories of the new unfold,
In vanguard visions, truth is told.

The pioneers of fleeting dreams,
Across the currents, through the streams,
They light the path with golden beams,
Echoing their vanguard themes.

Threads of Change

In the weave of time, they find their place,
Threads of change in woven grace,
A tapestry, each line a trace,
Of worlds evolved, a new embrace.

From ancient looms to modern hands,
They stretch across a hundred lands,
Symbols etched in shifting sands,
Threads of change form vibrant strands.

With colors bright and patterns vast,
They tell our future, speak our past,
Through gentle weave and shadow cast,
They bind us firm, yet flow so fast.

In silent strength, they weave and bind,
The hopes of all, the humankind,
In every thread, a tale enshrined,
Threads of change are paths aligned.

As loom and shuttle dance their art,
They craft a whole from parts apart,
Building bridges in the heart,
Threads of change, a timeless chart.

Pathways of Tomorrow

Beyond the crest of evening's glow,
Lies the land where dreams do grow,
Pathways leading soft and slow,
Into futures yet to know.

Steps we take in dawn's embrace,
Through vast expanses, open space,
New beginnings interlace,
Pathways of tomorrow trace.

With faith as guide and hope as hand,
Across the seas, o'er shifting sands,
We journey through uncharted lands,
Pathways molding future plans.

Light of wisdom, beacon bright,
Illuminates through darkest night,
Every choice adds to the sight,
Of pathways leading to new heights.

In every heart a vision's seed,
Paths of courage, paths of need,
With each step, our souls are freed,
Pathways of tomorrow lead.

Cipher of Creativity

Whispers in the silent mind,
Threads of thought, they come unlined.
Waves of ink on parchment flows,
Seeds of wonder, dreams bestows.

Painted realms in vivid hue,
Brush of time, creation's cue.
From chaos, patterns crystallize,
Vision's flare, it mystifies.

Each new stroke, a daring leap,
Through dark voids, ideas seep.
Labyrinths of unseen art,
Finds its voice, a burning start.

In the forge where muses sing,
Boundless lore they often bring.
Echoes of a distant spark,
Guide the way, consume the dark.

With each verse, and each refrain,
Sprouts a bloom, escapes the chain.
Ciphered thoughts transform the night,
Creativity takes its flight.

Unlocking the Unseen

Keys of thought in darkness kept,
Behind the eyes where dreams have slept.
Mystic doors, they slowly creak,
To realms unknown, whispers speak.

Beneath the veil of waking's mask,
Lies the realm where secrets bask.
Silent shadows full of might,
Reveal themselves in morning light.

Dreams entwined with strands of fate,
Patterns subtle, delicate.
Unlocking through the mind’s deep vault,
Ways unseen, without halt.

What is hidden, shall be found,
In silent whispers, lost is bound.
Boundaries shatter, paths reveal,
In secret truths, a hidden zeal.

With courage drawn from inner sight,
We pierce the dark, embrace the light.
Unlocking what was once unseen,
We find the truth in what’s between.

Chains of Light

Bound by gleams of silver streams,
Through the night, they weave our dreams.
Chains of light from yonder star,
Hold us close, yet take us far.

In the web of fate and chance,
Forms a tether, starts a dance.
Kindling sparks that guide our way,
Night transforms to break of day.

Wrapped within this gentle bind,
Wisdom, power intertwined.
Echoed glow from time gone by,
Lights the path where shadows lie.

Brilliant bonds, they do not break,
Strengthened with each step we take.
Hand in hand with radiant thread,
Leads where fears no longer tread.

Chains of light, though hold us tight,
Grant us wings for boundless flight.
Bound in freedom's luminous grace,
Shapes our journey, sets our pace.

Symphony of Breakthroughs

Echoes of a distant chord,
Strike the keys where dreams accord.
Notes of triumph, clear and bright,
Fill the dawn with pure delight.

Rising from the silent dark,
Clarity ignites a spark.
Melody of truth and skill,
Conquering each daunting hill.

Every challenge, every strain,
Feeds the rhythm, sweet refrain.
Harmony from strife is born,
Crafting futures, newly sworn.

Symphony that breaks our chains,
Cheers the soul, endures the pains.
In each verse, a new embrace,
Paves the way through time and space.

Revel in the sound's ascent,
In each whisper, joy is sent.
Who could fathom such a song?
Yet in each heart, it sings along.

Visionary Veins

In the quiet hum of night, we trace,
The dreams that flutter with gentle grace,
Painted in starlit, intricate designs,
Our visionary veins entwined in lines.

Through shadows cast by fleeting time,
We sculpt our future in rhythmic rhyme,
Echoes of hopes, in soft refrain,
Reside within our visionary vein.

With every pulse, a new dawn springs,
Imagination in every heartstring clings,
Breathing life into uncharted plains,
We find strength in visionary veins.

Beneath the canvas of moonlit beams,
Unfurled are threads of silken dreams,
Woven with whispers of the unseen,
Visionary veins in twilight gleam.

In the essence of each thought bestowed,
A tapestry of potential glowed,
Bound by the light that hope sustains,
Coursing through visionary veins.

Catalysts in Motion

In the heart of the storm, we ignite,
Flickers of change in the velvet night,
Movements stirring from the deep,
Catalysts in motion, never asleep.

A whisper turns into a thunderous call,
Breaking through the barriers tall,
Shifting tides, altering the oceans,
We are the catalysts, set in motion.

Ripples turned waves, in forceful sway,
Challenging norms with every ray,
Momentum built from sparks unseen,
Catalysts in motion, a boundless dream.

Through uncharted realms, we surge,
Creating paths where none converge,
Echoes of progress in every stride,
Catalysts in motion, side by side.

Unyielding, with purpose in our veins,
Forging futures where hope reigns,
In the dance of perpetual devotion,
We are the catalysts in endless motion.

Embryo of Ideas

Within the cradle of minds unformed,
Ideas spark and a world transformed,
Quiet embers of thought ignite,
The embryo of ideas takes flight.

In a realm of limitless potential,
Each spark of thought quintessential,
Birthing dreams from shadows and light,
In the embryo of ideas’ might.

Soft murmurs crafted into bold scream,
From the subconscious, a vivid dream,
Every concept a seedling sown,
In the fertile fields of the unknown.

Tenderly nurtured in silent care,
Visions emerge from mere air,
Growing stronger with the dawn,
Embryo of ideas, endlessly drawn.

Entwined with passion and desire,
A symphony within, born of fire,
Infinite roads from a single spark,
Embryo of ideas lighting the dark.

Wings of Modernity

In neon lights and digital streams,
Modernity soars on silicon dreams,
Woven threads of bytes and code,
Upon wings of modernity, we rode.

Through fiber veins, we weave and flight,
Our futures written in binary light,
A symphony of progress in each stride,
Wings of modernity, how wide they glide.

Embracing the future, a boundless sky,
Where circuits hum and data flies,
Bound by innovation, cutting seams,
We soar on the wings of modern dreams.

Connections forged through unseen ways,
In this era of radiant displays,
Our voices echo in digital scenes,
On the wings of modernity's pristine.

Blending the old with future's core,
Creating realms unseen before,
With every leap, a new reality,
We soar on wings of modernity.

Virtuoso of Vision

In the realm where thought ignites,
A spark becomes creation's spree.
Beyond the veils of mundane blight,
Rises an artist, wild and free.

Mirrors of dreams, they paint in air,
Colors seen by verdant heart.
Each stroke, a whisper, faint yet rare,
Echoes of an ancient start.

Stars and echoes, realms entwined,
Canvas kissed by cosmic grace.
Through the shadow, light confined,
Glimpse of eternity in space.

Vibrant hues of time, unfurled,
Metaphors in twilight's glow.
Virtuoso's visions, skies of pearl,
Beyond what words could ever show.

Beacon's Edge

Upon the precipice of night,
A lantern beams through shadow’s dread.
Guiding souls with silken light,
A beacon's edge where fears are shed.

Waves whisper tales of dusk and dawn,
Harbingers of secret lore.
In twilight’s cloak, illusions drawn,
Reveal the path to evermore.

Footprints fade on sands of time,
Moments lost to ocean’s sigh.
Yet through the dark, the beacon's chime,
Calls the weary, bids them fly.

Celestial orbs in spectral dance,
Silent guardians of the deep.
At beacon’s edge, hope finds a chance,
In dreams the heart shall safely keep.

Whirlwind of Whimsy

In the land where laughter reigns,
Winds of joy commence their spin.
Through the valleys, down the plains,
Whirlwind of whimsy shall begin.

Clouds of candy, skies of play,
Rainbows arch in endless sweep.
Every moment, a ballet,
In this realm where wonders leap.

Dandelions float on breeze,
Petals scattered, dancing free.
Through the giggles, through the tease,
Nature’s handcrafts glee's decree.

Children's laughter, pure and bright,
Magic in each fleeting glance.
Whirlwind's spins, both day and night,
Life's delightful, dreamy trance.

Gears of Imagination

In the realm of the unseen,
Where dreams forever dance,
Imagination's gears convene,
To give us hope and chance.

With every turn, new worlds appear,
Of kingdoms yet unsung,
Where courage fights off fear,
And songs of hearts are sprung.

Bold ideas, crisp and fresh,
Take flight on airy wings,
Innovation starts to mesh,
Inspired by simple things.

The mind, a clockwork grand,
Spins tales both wild and bright,
Building castles out of sand,
In the soft-hued twilight.

Where reality and dreams align,
The magic starts to stir,
In the gears of the divine,
Life's fantasies confer.

Beyond Boundaries

Eyes set on the distant haze,
Traversing through the mist,
In endless, winding maze,
New worlds wait to be kissed.

Silent whispers call our name,
From places far and wide,
Undaunted by the claim,
We step beyond and glide.

Boundaries merely lines we draw,
To cage our wandering minds,
But with courage as our law,
Freedom and truth we find.

Through forests dense and seas so vast,
Our spirits seek to soar,
Carving paths from future to past,
Discovering ever more.

In uncharted, wild terrain,
Awaits the boundless feast,
A freedom we can only gain,
When boundaries are released.

Nurturing the New

Tender sprouts of fragile green,
Emerging from the earth,
Within them lies unseen,
Potential's mighty worth.

Nurturing dreams to full bloom,
With sunlight and with care,
Through storm, sun, and gloomy gloom,
Hope rises everywhere.

The cradle of an open mind,
A garden for the youth,
Truth in discoveries we find,
Amongst the seeds of truth.

Fostering the bold and bright,
In fields of boundless hue,
Each spirit taking flight,
In the nurturing of the new.

With patience and gentle hand,
We mold the future dawn,
Leaving footprints in the sand,
Till a fresh day is born.

Waves of Thought

Across the sea of endless mind,
Waves of thought do lie,
In each crest, a tale we find,
Of dreams that never die.

Subtle whispers of the deep,
Carried on the breeze,
In secrets that the oceans keep,
Ideas find their ease.

Moments lost in swirling tides,
Chasing after time,
In the ebb, new hope resides,
Each wave a silent rhyme.

Flowing currents strong and free,
Drift through endless night,
In the waves of thought we see,
The dawn of pure insight.

The ocean vast of human lore,
Holds wisdom's hidden gems,
Waves of thought forevermore,
On starlit diadems.

Inventors' Realm

In a world where dreams ignite,
Shapes and sounds take flight.
Visionaries craft with zeal,
Imagination, passion's real.

From spark of thought, marvels rise,
Rainbows cast in midnight skies.
Creations woven from bold thread,
Future drawn from paths they tread.

In labs, in minds, they design,
Bringing forth the grand divine.
Tiny cogs of our advance,
On this stage, their hearts dance.

Beyond the known, they roam afar,
Chasing every distant star.
Inventors’ realm, where wonders flow,
Seeds of hope they gladly sow.

Boundless visions reach their prime,
Through the endless stretch of time.
They're the architects of change,
In the dreamscape, minds arrange.

Trailblazing Minds

Minds that breach the veils unseen,
Trailblazers where none had been.
Carving roads in rough terrain,
Through the joy and through the pain.

Ideas bright as fields of gold,
Yield the tales yet to be told.
Courage mixed with wisdom rare,
Guiding all with strength to dare.

Pioneers with hearts so bold,
Mysteries of life unfold.
Charting paths so others see,
Ways to be and ways to free.

Innovation's fearless dance,
Taking every daring chance.
Exploring wonders, boundless land,
Together, hand in trusting hand.

Every mind a boundless sea,
Flowing bright with energy.
Trailblazing in a realm so vast,
Forging futures from the past.

Eternal Quest

In search of truth, the quest began,
Through the realms unknown to man.
Endless paths and oceans wide,
Stars as guides and dreams inside.

Seeking wisdom, boundless, free,
In the heart of mystery.
Every step brings new insight,
Through the depths of endless night.

Curiosity, the driving force,
Guiding through a winding course.
Quests for answers, hearts afire,
Journeys filled with bright desire.

Through the sands of time they tread,
Following where thoughts are led.
Bound by neither earth nor sky,
Reaching far where shadows lie.

Eternal quest, it never ends,
In the cosmos, light extends.
Searching for the unknown shore,
The spirit's call to seek once more.

Breakthrough Horizons

On the brink of dawn anew,
Horizons vast come into view.
Breakthroughs birthed from minds so bright,
Kindling hope, dispelling night.

Boundaries pushed where none have dared,
Every dream and vision shared.
Pioneers of thought and deed,
Planting every fertile seed.

In the crucible of change,
Ideas meld and rearrange.
Innovation's light so near,
Casts aside the darkest fear.

Waves of progress never cease,
From the struggle, sweet release.
Through the storm, a beacon's gleam,
Guiding all with fervent beam.

Horizons break with morning's kiss,
In each heart, a boundless bliss.
Together rise, a dawn reborn,
On breakthrough's path, a new world sworn.

The Creator's Code

In circuits bright, the data streams,
Within the chips, the coded dreams.
A spark ignites the crafted lore,
Each byte, a key to open doors.

Algorithms, in quiet run,
Crafting wonders, one by one.
In silent hums, the future grows,
From ones and zeroes, truth bestows.

A language born of clicks and clacks,
With logic pure, no need for hacks.
Infinite loops, commands precise,
Figures dance in coded splice.

Within the heart of silicon,
A symphony of truth's begun.
Craftsmen of the digital age,
Write the codes on endless page.

In user’s touch, the code unfolds,
A universe within behold.
Crafted by the hands unseen,
Builders of the new machine.

Bridges to Beyond

Across the void, through spans of thought,
New realms of wonder we have sought.
From ancient shores to modern heights,
We bridge the worlds with boundless flights.

Steel and stone, but more than mere,
Connections forged, horizons clear.
Through webs of light and lines of code,
New paths into the vast explode.

Traversing through the unknown skies,
Our visions reach where darkness lies.
Each step a daring, heart-felt leap,
To mysteries in shadows deep.

From deep below to stars above,
Bridges built with dreams and love.
Beyond the known, our souls are led,
To futures vast and lightly tread.

In steps untrodden, faith is found,
In silent whispers, dreams unbound.
We cross the gaps, with courage shown,
To worlds and wonders still unknown.

Techne's Touch

In iron hands, the craft begins,
With each new pulse, a world spins.
From circuits born of ancient lore,
Technology's touch opens doors.

Mechanics fused with whispers old,
In coded lines, stories told.
From heart of gears, the spirit flows,
In digital breath, life bestows.

Whence came the touch of human craft,
The echo of the ages graft?
In seamless bonds of mind and hand,
Our future sculpted grains of sand.

Creations grand in form and mind,
Each thought and thread with purpose bind.
In technic arms, we saw our pride,
The tools to worlds, by none denied.

In reverence to the past we climb,
Within its grasp, the sands of time.
The dance of craft, both new and old,
Techne’s touch, in future, bold.

Embers of Discovery

In darkened skies, a spark ignites,
A beacon bright in endless nights.
With every flame, a truth revealed,
In embers, secrets long concealed.

From ancient stars, the whispers sigh,
In cosmic threads, the answers lie.
With telescope and deepened gaze,
We pierce the vast, the cosmic maze.

Each ember holds a story old,
Of distant worlds and tales untold.
With science as our guiding light,
We journey forth into the night.

Through lens and scope our dreams we chase,
In quest to understand our place.
In embers bright, the fire grows,
A universe, its secrets shows.

In fires faint but ever near,
We find the truth, the cosmic cheer.
Embers of discovery, brightly gleam,
In endless quest, the human dream.

Echoes of Tomorrow

In the silence of today,
We hear whispers of a dawn,
A promise not yet made,
An echo not yet drawn.

Paths we are yet to follow,
Footsteps etched in air,
Promises of tomorrow,
In shadows, they do flare.

Sunrise yet unseen,
Kisses the morning dew,
Tomorrow's hidden dream,
In colors bold and true.

A whisper through the trees,
Leaves dancing in the wind,
Echoes of tomorrow's breeze,
Where new worlds begin.

The night shall soon depart,
The day begins to glow,
Tomorrow's beating heart,
In whispers soft and slow.

Blueprint of Dreams

Dreams woven in the night,
Blueprints of our soul,
In shadows soft and light,
Where visions make us whole.

Stars above do guide,
Through darkness, they will gleam,
A universe inside,
The blueprint of a dream.

Lines drawn in twilight's hue,
Sketches of a world anew,
In every shade and blue,
Awaken to the view.

Pages of unspoken lore,
Blueprints whispering near,
Dreams forever more,
In sketches crystal clear.

Hearts and minds align,
In the silence, they convene,
Blueprints intertwine,
In the architecture of a dream.

Minds Unchained

In a world unbound,
Minds reach to the sky,
Chains fall to the ground,
Dreams begin to fly.

Ideas start to bloom,
In gardens vast and wide,
Minds break free from gloom,
In freedom they confide.

Walls dissolve to dust,
Horizons bold and new,
In dreams, we place our trust,
To selves forever true.

Creativity takes flight,
In colors wild and free,
Minds born of pure light,
Embrace infinity.

Boundaries fade away,
With every thought we find,
A brand new world each day,
In the freedom of the mind.

Seeds of the Future

In earth rich and deep,
We plant tomorrow’s seed,
Dreams awake from sleep,
To flourish and to lead.

The future yet to unfold,
In tendrils reaching high,
Promises of gold,
In the vast, open sky.

Nurtured by the rain,
And kissed by morning’s light,
Dreams grow to sustain,
Through each passing night.

Branches twist and turn,
In the dance of the breeze,
Life lessons we learn,
In the whisper of the trees.

From seed to mighty tree,
The future's dream takes hold,
A legacy to be,
In stories yet untold.

New Dawn Rising

Beneath the canopy of night,
Stars weave tales of distant lands,
A whisper grows, forsakes the dark,
With morning's touch, dreams expand.

Sunlight kisses dewdrops bright,
Hope's petals unfurl anew,
Awoken world, breathe in the light,
A canvas fresh, skies of blue.

Mountains greet with gentle glow,
Birdsongs herald day's embrace,
In shadows long, the embers glow,
Pursuits of joy in every space.

Horizons gilded with rebirth,
Promises of journeys far,
The heart awakes, discarding mirth,
As dawn ascends, a guiding star.

Paths unfold in hues sublime,
Echoes of nocturnal sighs,
Rise above in rhythm and rhyme,
A new dawn in the joyful skies.

Born of Curiosity

Eyes wide in wonder, minds aflame,
Questions sprout, a boundless sea,
Whispers call from realms untamed,
Born of curiosity, we're free.

Beneath the surface, treasures lie,
Hidden truths in silent codes,
Through layers deep, we seek, we pry,
Journeying along knowledge's roads.

Each step a revelation found,
In labyrinths of thought profound,
A universe in whispers bound,
Its mystic secrets to astound.

Imagination leads our quest,
Venturing beyond the known,
In curiosity, we are blessed,
Seeds of wisdom's garden sown.

So let this flame within us burn,
Unyielding in its fervent flight,
For in each twist and curious turn,
We carve our path in endless light.

Waves of Genius

Ideas crash on minds' vast shores,
Tides of brilliance ever flow,
In every swell, the spirit soars,
In ceaseless waves of genius grow.

Inspired thoughts, like currents, run,
From ocean depths to surface clear,
In every crest, a daunting sun,
Bright insights in their radiant sphere.

Innovation rides the breeze,
On whispers of the unknown winds,
With sails of dreams, we cross the seas,
Enlightenment's quest begins.

Horizons teeming with the spark,
Of answers waiting to be found,
With every wave, through light and dark,
In mind's expanse, uncharted ground.

Let brilliance guide our wayward ships,
Through tempests wild and tranquil peace,
For in the waves of genius' grips,
We find the path to sweetest release.

Behind the Spark

Moments fleeting, yet they last,
Through the veils of time unseen,
Behind the spark, a shadow cast,
Of dreams that could have never been.

The flash of thought, a silent muse,
In the dark, it plays its part,
Leaving trails of varied hues,
Etched deeply in the human heart.

The fleeting glow of silent mind,
In a realm of endless night,
Behind the spark, the truth we find,
Illuminated by its light.

In whispers soft, the ember speaks,
Of tales untold, yet to arise,
Behind the spark, the spirit seeks,
Visions hidden from plain eyes.

So cherish every spark within,
As fleeting moments intertwine,
For in its glow, our fates begin,
Bound forever, by design.

Pioneer's Palette

In realms where shadows softly blend,
The dreams of pioneers ascend.
Brush strokes paint the unknown skies,
With colors bold that mesmerize.

A canvas vast, uncharted space,
They stride with hope and measured pace.
In every hue, a story told,
Of courage bright and ventures bold.

From dusk till dawn, their visions burn,
In twilight's glow, they discern.
New worlds await their tender touch,
Transforming void with every brush.

The palette held by daring hands,
Ignites the night in distant lands.
In galaxies where starlight weeps,
Their legacy in silence keeps.

Seek not the easy path to stay,
For pioneers craft a brighter way.
Their colors vivid, pure, and true,
Cast dreams upon the ever blue.

Dreamscapes Defined

In midnight's hush, our dreams take flight,
Waltzing through the realms of night.
Ethereal paths by moonlight lined,
Reveal the dreams our hearts have signed.

Stars whisper tales in silver tones,
Of lands unseen, with gold-lit stones.
Each dreamscape forged with light so kind,
Carries the hopes we've left behind.

Through valleys veiled in sapphire mist,
Where echoes of our visions twist.
An odyssey on wings confined,
Explores the depths of the defined.

Each dawn we wake, our dreams disperse,
But linger soft in quiet verse.
Fragments of the night unwind,
Leaving traces intertwined.

With every dream, we redefine,
The boundaries of the soul's design.
In the night, our spirits bind,
Hopes and dreams, forever signed.

Quantum Quests

Within the fabric of the night,
Particles dance in cosmic light.
Dimensions weave through spacetime's threads,
Where quantum quests by minds are led.

A quark's embrace, a photon's kiss,
In realms of mysteries, abyss.
Velocities in silence swept,
Where secrets of the void are kept.

Wavefunctions whisper, secrets told,
Of universes yet to mold.
In dance of particles, entwine,
The essence of the grand design.

Entanglements of fate and force,
Guide the quantum's hidden course.
Through realms unseen by waking eyes,
The truth within the question lies.

Explore the quantum world profound,
Where paradoxes pale surround.
In every quantum leap and jest,
Seek the heart of the cosmic quest.

New Age Nectar

Beneath the skies of digital dawn,
A nectar new, the world is drawn.
Bytes and codes in streams align,
Crafting futures intertwined.

In circuits' hum, where dreams arise,
A new age forms before our eyes.
With silicon and light's embrace,
We carve our path through boundless space.

Whispers of a world anew,
In data’s dance, our visions grew.
A tapestry of pixels bright,
Guides us through the endless night.

Yet in the tech, a heart remains,
A pulse of life in digital veins.
The nectar sweet of progress pure,
Promises tomorrows sure.

Embrace the new with open arms,
Savor the age with all its charms.
For in its flow, we find our place,
A future forged in boundless grace.

Engines of Evolution

In depths of time, where shadows sway,
Engines churned, and life found way.
From primal ooze to skies above,
With every spark, a world to love.

Hands of fate, a cosmic dance,
Through the ages, life’s advance.
Atoms fused and stars begot,
Dreams from dust, in webs were caught.

Nature's pulse, a rhythmic beat,
Mountains rise and plates retreat.
Forests burgeon, deserts bloom,
In the spiral, there's always room.

From scales to wings, and fur to feather,
Diverse forms yet knit together.
Survival sings in every kind,
Evolution, an untamed mind.

Mysterious force, unseen embrace,
Guiding life through time and space.
Engines hum, ever in motion,
Crafting worlds with pure devotion.

Neon Dreams

City lights that paint the night,
Neon whispers, soft and bright.
Streetlights hum, and shadows play,
In dreams of color, night will sway.

Electric hum beneath skin,
Neon streets, where dreamers spin.
Hopes ignite in purple haze,
Lost in beauty, minds ablaze.

In alleys deep, where secrets lie,
Neon dreams soars to sky.
Glowing signs, a symphony,
Life in neon, wild and free.

Reflections in the midnight glass,
Future’s promise, shadows pass.
Neon pathways, unknown trails,
Guiding hearts on astral sails.

Cosmic dreams in neon's glow,
Boundless as the rivers flow.
Crimson, violet, indigo,
In city’s heart, dreams ebb and flow.

Pulse of Potential

Silent whispers in the dawn,
Potential bursts as day is born.
Hopeful hearts, with dreams to weave,
Endless pathways, to believe.

Boundless skies, uncharted flight,
Vision’s edge, the heart ignites.
Creeds of courage, strength revealed,
In pulse of life, our fates are sealed.

Seeds of thought in fertile mind,
Creations bloom where we’re inclined.
Innovation’s earnest plea,
To transform naught to something free.

Every breath a promise new,
Opportunities in view.
Galaxies within our reach,
Through endless learning, others teach.

The pulse of potential, ever strong,
In every heart, its timeless song.
Together, paths unknown we pave,
In unity, the boundless brave.

Seeds and Circuits

In fertile soil, the seeds we sow,
Nature’s code, in rhythm flow.
Life and tech, a fusion bright,
Circuits hum in starlit night.

Roots entwine with wired veins,
Organic minds and silicon brains.
Future’s promise holds us tight,
In seeds and circuits, hope ignites.

Growth in silicon and earth,
Binary dreams that find their birth.
Echoes blend of past and new,
Nature's song in digital hue.

Green and glowing, fields converge,
Interfaces on life’s verge.
Together, merging earth and sky,
In seeds and circuits, futures lie.

A dance of ages, old and young,
Nature’s verses digitally sung.
Bound in harmony, we strive,
Seeds and circuits, come alive.

Beyond the Known

In the twilight of mind's endless sea,
Where shadows and dreams intertwine,
We venture to realms yet unseen,
Journeying through space and time.

Stars whisper secrets untold,
Galaxies dance in silent embrace,
Boundaries of the cosmos unfold,
Revealing infinity's grace.

Among constellations we wander,
Seekers of the obscure and rare,
In the vastness, hearts grow fonder,
For mysteries that drift in the air.

To brave the abyss, we yearn,
With courage in our souls alight,
The unknown beckons, paths to discern,
Guided by the stars' gentle light.

So we'll chart the skies with wonder,
Beyond the known, our spirits roam,
In the cosmic symphony, no sunder,
Finding in the vast expanse our home.

Visionary Paths

Winding roads through forests of thought,
Where whispers of wisdom softly call,
Each step on dreams and visions caught,
Guides us beneath the canopy tall.

Lanterns of hope line the way,
Casting shadows upon ancient lore,
In twilight's embrace, shadows sway,
Revealing doors to what lies before.

Voices of past and future blend,
In the chorus of the present song,
Through hidden trails our spirits wend,
Towards realms where we belong.

Markers of time sculpt the stones,
In the pathways of the surreal,
Through visionary paths, all alone,
The secret world to heal.

With every breath, a mystery untwined,
On roads where the sun and moon shine,
We walk the visionary paths, unconfined,
Our destinies forever intertwined.

Unseen Frontiers

Beneath horizons veiled in mist,
Beyond the realms of sight,
Lie frontiers that persist,
In the dance of day to night.

Mountains rise in ghostly swells,
Oceans whisper lost refrains,
Through the unseen, a story tells,
Of ancient suns and sacred rains.

Caverns echo silent hymns,
Stars ignite the distant skies,
In these frontiers, the light dims,
Yet within, true wisdom lies.

Through deserts of the unknown,
Across the seas of mystic gray,
Unseen frontiers have ever grown,
Guiding seekers on their way.

In the heart of endless reaches,
Where the unseen becomes clear,
We discover what life teaches,
Beyond the veil of frontier.

Eureka Moments

A spark within the dark,
Illuminating midnight's veil,
Eureka calls, a sudden lark,
Revelations bold and frail.

In whispered thoughts they lie,
Glimmers in the ocean's sweep,
Like stars within the cobalt sky,
Awake from moment's sleep.

A flash of insight’s fire,
Ignites the seeker’s quest,
Turning doubts to pure desire,
In truth, our souls invest.

Elusive dreams take form,
With clarity they swiftly soar,
Through the eye of the storm,
We find reality to explore.

With every light discovered,
New paths to us unfolds,
Eureka moments, cherished, recovered,
Stories of the brave retold.

Echoes of Eureka

In twilight's hush, ideas take flight,
Whispers of wonder, a spark's delight.
Silent musings, in shadows play,
Echoes of Eureka, night to day.

Labyrinths of the mind, so vast,
Conceived in moments that rush past.
Silent symphonies, wisdom sings,
In the chamber of thought, dreams take wings.

A flicker, a flame, a light bestowed,
Knowledge, once hidden, now unfolds.
From depths unseen, revelations rise,
In a dance of stars, across the skies.

Unraveling threads, a tapestry bright,
The quest for truth, an endless flight.
In every heart, in every mind,
Echoes of Eureka, treasures we find.

In quiet reflection, answers appear,
Guided by intuition, dispelling fear.
From spark to blaze, visions bloom,
In the sacred space of our inner room.

Architects of Awakening

Beneath the starry canopy, we dream,
Crafting futures from hope's gleam.
Building bridges, heart to heart,
Architects of awakening, worlds to start.

With every stone of truth we lay,
Structures of awareness, night and day.
Foundations firm, of love and trust,
In unity, we'll rise from dust.

Blueprints drawn in cosmic sand,
Guided by an unseen hand.
In every soul, a universe, vast,
Awakening dawns, shadows cast.

Through trials faced, and battles fought,
Together in spirit, lessons taught.
In shared purpose, we align,
Architects of awakening, designs divine.

In harmony, our dreams converge,
Bound by an ethereal surge.
Creating realms where hearts are free,
Awakened by love, eternally.

Curiosity's Crusade

A spark ignites the soul's quest,
Beyond the horizon, no longer at rest.
Curiosity, the guiding light,
Leads the crusade through endless night.

Mysteries woven in each star,
In every question, near or far.
With open minds, we seek, we find,
Truths entangled, yet aligned.

Boundaries blurred in pursuit's gleam,
Reality mingles with the dream.
Across the fields of time we bound,
Curiosity's echoes, all around.

Each step graced by knowledge's touch,
In small discoveries, the world is such.
An endless journey, no path defined,
A mosaic of thoughts, intertwined.

With every answer, deeper we delve,
In the labyrinth of self, we evolve.
Crusaders of understanding, undismayed,
Onward, ever onward, Curiosity's crusade.

Odyssey of the New

Set sail on seas of uncharted blue,
Ventures bold, and dreams anew.
Horizons beckon, unseen lands,
Odyssey of the new, in our hands.

With hearts as compasses, we steer,
Through storms and calms, far and near.
Each wave, a challenge, each breeze, a guide,
In discovery's embrace, we abide.

Journeys penned in stardust ink,
Destinies sculpted, on the brink.
Pathways forge beneath our stride,
With courage and wonder, worlds collide.

Every dawn reveals a fresh terrain,
From mountaintops to endless plain.
In the whispers of the morning dew,
An odyssey unfolds, always new.

In every heartbeat, an adventure starts,
Echoed in the rhythm of our hearts.
Guided by visions, we pursue,
Eternal travelers, Odyssey of the new.

Voyage of Verve

Set sail on waves of dreams, through skies azure,
With courage as our guide, and heart for sure.
Whispers of winds through sails, our spirits steer,
A voyage of verve, where no shadows sneer.

Stars sprinkle wisdom, ancient paths they draw,
In the tapestry of night, our vessel's awe.
Echoes of sailors past, in moon's embrace,
Guiding our journey, with a timeless grace.

Through storms of doubt, and oceans deep of fear,
The compass of resolve, forever near.
Horizons kissed by dawn, in hues so bold,
A voyage of verve, with stories yet untold.

From ports unknown to shores of golden gleam,
Our souls awaken to the boundless dream.
With every wave, a whisper 'cross the seas,
A symphony of courage, in every breeze.

Anchored not by fate, but choice we weave,
In each horizon's arms, a chance to believe.
The voyage of verve, embraced by the free,
Adrift in passion's sea, eternally.

Sculptors of Serenity

Hands of grace, crafting peace divine,
In marble veins, a tranquil sign.
Chiseling chaos, molding time's embrace,
Sculptors of serenity, in every space.

Monuments of stillness, stand so stark,
In tranquil gardens, where souls embark.
Each touch a symphony of calm so pure,
In silence, life’s whispers they procure.

Veins of stone, with heartbeat’s gentle tone,
Resonating peace, where light has shone.
Every carve, a story to unfold,
Of serenity, in hearts to hold.

From chaos birthed, to harmony's state,
In the sculptor's grasp, a peaceful fate.
Fragment by fragment, peace they decree,
Sculptors of serenity, eternally free.

In the sanctum of stillness they confide,
With every piece, a tranquil tide.
Their art transforms, and minds set free,
Sculptors of serenity, through divinity.

Beyond the Brilliance

In twilight's embrace, the stars paint dreams,
Beyond the brilliance, where silence beams.
A canvas vast, of endless night,
Where whispering winds bestow their light.

Celestial wonders, in quiet glow,
Illuminate paths where dreams will flow.
Constellations guide hearts, unconfined,
In the realm of thoughts, we seek and find.

Through cosmic veils, our spirits soar,
Past brilliance bold, to realms of lore.
Nebulae dance in a symphony true,
In the vast expanse, a world anew.

Transcend the mundane, to astral seas,
Where every thought is a universe's key.
In silence profound, we find profound grace,
Beyond the brilliance, in endless space.

In the gardens of stars, our minds take flight,
Unveiling the mysteries cloaked in night.
A realm where dreams and reality blend,
Beyond the brilliance, where infinities extend.

Harbingers of Hopes

In dawn's early light, they softly tread,
Harbingers of hopes, where fears have fled.
With wings of resilience, through skies they glide,
Woven from dreams, with hearts open wide.

Songs of tomorrow, they gently sing,
In every note, new beginnings bring.
Guiding the weary through night's embrace,
To mornings of promise, with radiant grace.

Beneath their touch, despair turns to bloom,
In fields of future, dispelling gloom.
Harbingers of hopes, in whispers mild,
Cradle our sorrows, with spirit beguiled.

Through storms of doubt, they pierce the veil,
With light of optimism, they prevail.
In every shadow, their presence felt,
Turning cold stone, to warmth where we've knelt.

Messengers of love, in every hue,
With wings outstretched, they guide us through.
The harbingers of hopes, timeless and true,
In their embrace, all dreams renew.

Creators' Codex

In ink and thought, the codex grows,
A world of dreams and endless flows.
From mind to page, creation springs,
Imagination takes its wings.

Each stroke reveals a hidden lore,
Unseen realms behind the door.
Words entwine in secret dance,
A universe within a glance.

Builders of realms, we hold the key,
Crafting futures yet to see.
A codex of the life we mold,
In silent pages, tales untold.

Mysteries decoded line by line,
Infinite is the grand design.
A legacy in every script,
Eternal truths our pens have writ.

With every thought, the codex grows,
A timeless tapestry, we compose.
The ink of life within our hold,
Creators' tales will soon unfold.

Lanterns of Lucidity

Amidst the night's soft velvet hue,
Lanterns glimmer into view.
Guiding souls with gentle light,
Through the corridors of night.

Clarity in every glow,
Where dreams and truths begin to show.
A beacon in the darkest times,
Echoes of the ancient chimes.

In gleaming orbs of soft embrace,
Wisdom lights each shadowed space.
A journey through the realms of thought,
Where lucidity is sought.

Stars align with lantern's gleam,
Whispering secrets in a dream.
Mind and soul in perfect sync,
In their glow, we find the link.

These lanterns shine in endless sky,
A bridge between the earth and high.
Lucid paths they trace and roam,
Leading us to find our home.

Prisms of Potential

In every heart lies hidden light,
A spectrum vast, both day and night.
Prisms of potential gleam,
Manifested from a dream.

Colors burst from deep inside,
In every shade, our paths collide.
A mosaic of our hopes and fears,
Reflecting brilliance through the years.

Infinite in every hue,
Possibilities anew.
Each direction, every choice,
Echoed in the silent voice.

From shards of doubt to beams of grace,
We find our unique place.
A journey through the spectrum wide,
Where potentials brightly hide.

Prisms casting vibrant rays,
Infinite in countless ways.
Within the light, our truth distills,
A tapestry of endless thrills.

Waves of Wonder

By the shore, where day meets night,
Waves of wonder catch the light.
Infinite in their embrace,
Crashing in a timeless grace.

Whispers of the ocean's song,
In the waves, we find where we belong.
Rolling rhythm of the deep,
In their arms, our dreams they keep.

Each wave a tale, both old and new,
Carrying secrets, whispering through.
The vast expanse of liquid sky,
Reflected in the ocean's eye.

Drenched in splendor, pure and wild,
Nature's heartbeat, soft and mild.
Cresting surges, ebbing flow,
In their dance, we come to know.

Waves of wonder call us near,
Murmuring what we need to hear.
In their depths, we are set free,
Boundless in their majesty.

Inventive Pulse

Invention starts with dreams anew,
In hearts where wonder grows,
A spark ignites, a vision true,
Where creativity flows.

In workshops bright, with minds so keen,
Ideas begin to fuse,
New paths are paved with sights unseen,
Imagination's muse.

Through trials faced and setbacks met,
The pulse of hope beats on,
For every challenge, no regret,
The dawn precedes the dawn.

From fleeting thoughts to crafted art,
The world is shaped and steered,
With every start, a brand-new part,
To futures yet endeared.

The pulse of invention never wanes,
It dances, leaps, and soars,
In every heart, in every brain,
The endless quest implores.

Journey Beyond Boundaries

Step beyond the edges known,
Into the great expanse,
With courage seed and spirit sown,
Embrace the boldest chance.

Through forests thick and deserts wide,
Across the mountains high,
We tread where none before had tried,
Beneath the open sky.

In quest for truth, in search of sight,
The journey takes its toll,
Yet every step through darkest night,
Illuminates the soul.

With maps uncharted, guides untamed,
We venture forth alone,
For in the heart of man inflamed,
The stars are brightly shown.

Beyond the bounds of what we know,
Lies a vast frontier,
In every step and wind's soft blow,
We find our purpose here.

Labyrinth of Discovery

Within the maze of thoughts so deep,
A labyrinth unseen,
Each turn a mystery to keep,
In minds where dreams convene.

Exploring depths of knowledge vast,
Designs and truths unfold,
Through every corridor we pass,
The future's tale is told.

In whispers soft and echoes clear,
In shadows and in light,
The path through wonder, void of fear,
Reveals new realms of sight.

Discoveries with each new bend,
Awakening the known,
The labyrinth begins to wend,
To places yet unshown.

In puzzles solved and riddles cracked,
In journeys near and far,
The labyrinth of mind intact,
Guides us to each star.

Whispers of Progress

In silent halls where shadows shift,
The whispers softly call,
Of moving forward, paths to lift,
Beyond the ancient thrall.

Progress hums in midnight air,
In factories and fields,
Through every effort made with care,
The future slowly yields.

From lab to street, from thinker's pen,
In whispers carried far,
The spark ignites in minds of men,
A dream like morning star.

Through trials faced and battles won,
Each whisper brings new light,
The dawn of progress just begun,
Dispel the darkest night.

With every step in silent stride,
The whispers, march, and call,
To new horizons, far and wide,
Where progress touches all.

Printed in the USA
CPSIA information can be obtained
at www.ICGtesting.com
LVHW050501260724
786473LV00002BA/197

9 789916 862711